100 WORDS TO MAKE YOU SOUND GREAT

THE 100 WORDS® *From the Editors of the*
AMERICAN HERITAGE®
DICTIONARIES

HOUGHTON MIFFLIN HARCOURT
Boston   New York

EDITORIAL STAFF OF THE
American Heritage® Dictionaries

MARGERY S. BERUBE, *Vice President, Publisher of Dictionaries*

JOSEPH P. PICKETT, *Vice President, Executive Editor*

STEVEN R. KLEINEDLER, *Supervising Editor*

SUSAN I. SPITZ, *Senior Editor*

CATHERINE T. PRATT, *Editor*

LOUISE E. ROBBINS, *Editor*

PATRICK TAYLOR, *Editor*

NICHOLAS A. DURLACHER, *Associate Editor*

PETER CHIPMAN, *Assistant Editor*

Visit our websites: www.ahdictionary.com
or www.hmhbooks.com

LIBRARY OF CONGRESS CATALOGING-IN-PUBLICATION DATA

100 words to make you sound great / from the editors of the American Heritage
dictionaries.
    p. cm. -- (100 words)
  Includes indexes.
  ISBN-13: 978-0-618-88310-3
  ISBN-10: 0-618-88310-X
 1. Quotations, English. I. Title: One hundred words to make you sound great.
  PN6081.A1256 2008
  081--dc22

2007034350

Text design by Anne Chalmers

MANUFACTURED IN THE UNITED STATES OF AMERICA
3 4 5 6 - EB - 15 14 13 12 11

Table of Contents

100 Words

to Make You

Sound Great

Preface

100 Words to Make You Sound Great is the eighth book
in the best-selling 100 Words series. The series high-
lights words that people who want to be taken seriously
ought to know and be able to put to good use.

After all, it is by words that problems get analyzed,
that new ideas are put forward and refined in the fur-
nace of critical thinking. Words are what we use to
make sense of our past, to comment on our present, to
envision our future. We use words to laugh at our-
selves, to get perspective, to resolve to do better.

The editors of the American Heritage dictionaries
have selected the words in this book as inspiring mod-
els in the effort of all communicators to be understood
and to be convincing. The words are defined in conven-
tional dictionary format and then shown in context
with quotations from some of our most important and
esteemed speakers and writers. Word origins are ex-
plained in etymologies, and on occasion fleshed out in
an explanatory note.

The communicators quoted in this book come from
all walks of life. They include politicians, social reform-
ers, economists, historians, scientists, essayists, cultural
commentators, humorists, and others. The words they
use are just as varied: powerful verbs (*beguile, supersede, wheedle*), striking nouns (*busybody, prescience,*

vista), and precise adjectives (*imperturbable, ludicrous, surreptitious*). They appear in famous speeches, in acclaimed histories, in award-winning books, in revealing letters.

We hope that readers will take up these words in their own efforts to be convincing as they engage in the noisy conversation we call the free exchange of ideas, because as the quotations in this book show, words really do make a difference.

— **Joseph Pickett,**
Executive Editor

Guide to the Entries

ENTRY WORDS The 100 words in this book are listed alphabetically. Each boldface entry word is followed by its pronunciation (see page ix for a pronunciation key) and at least one part of speech. One or more definitions are given for each part of speech with the central and most commonly sought sense first.

QUOTATIONS The editors chose quotations to encompass a wide spectrum of ideas and beliefs expressed by a diverse group of speakers and authors. These quotations illustrate how the entry words are actually used in speeches, books, articles, and essays.

ETYMOLOGIES (WORD HISTORIES) Etymologies appear in square brackets following the quotations. An etymology traces the history of a word as far back in time as can be determined with reasonable certainty. The stage most closely preceding Modern English is given first, with each earlier stage following in sequence. A language name, linguistic form (in italics), and brief definition of the form are given for each stage of the derivation presented. For reasons of space, the etymologies sometimes omit certain stages in the derivation of words with long and complex histories when this omission does not significantly detract from a broad understanding of the word's history. To avoid redundancy, a language, form, or definition is not repeated if it is identical to the corresponding item in the immediately preceding stage. The word *from* is used to indicate origin of any kind: by inheritance, borrowing, abbreviation, the addition of affixes, or any other linguistic process. When an etymology splits a compound word into parts, a colon comes after the compound word, and the parts (along with their histories in parentheses) follow in sequence linked by a plus sign (+). Occasionally, a form is given that is not actually preserved in written documents, but that scholars are confident did exist — such a form is marked by an asterisk (*).

NOTES Some entries include notes that present additional interesting information regarding the history of the word, including the process by which it entered English from other languages. These notes discuss the historical, cultural, or literary origins of the word and ways that it is used in addition to the senses that have been presented.

Pronunciation Guide

Pronunciations appear in parentheses after boldface entry words. If a word has more than one pronunciation, the first pronunciation is usually more common than the other, but often they are equally common. Pronunciations are shown after inflections and related words where necessary.

Stress is the relative degree of emphasis that a word's syllables are spoken with. An unmarked syllable has the weakest stress in the word. The strongest, or primary, stress is indicated with a bold mark (ˈ). A lighter mark (ˈ) indicates a secondary level of stress. The stress mark follows the syllable it applies to. Words of one syllable have no stress mark because there is no other stress level that the syllable can be compared to.

The key on page ix shows the pronunciation symbols used in this book. To the right of the symbols are words that show how the symbols are pronounced. The letters whose sound corresponds to the symbols are shown in boldface.

The symbol (ə) is called *schwa*. It represents a vowel with the weakest level of stress in a word. The schwa sound varies slightly according to the vowel it represents or the sounds around it:

a·bun·dant (ə-bŭnˈdənt)   **mo·ment** (mōˈmənt)

civ·il (sĭvˈəl)   **grate·ful** (grātˈfəl)

PRONUNCIATION KEY

Symbol	Examples	Symbol	Examples
ă	pat	oi	noise
ā	pay	ŏŏ	took
âr	care	ŏŏr	lure
ä	father	ōō	boot
b	bib	ou	out
ch	church	œ	*German* schön
d	deed, milled	p	pop
ĕ	pet	r	roar
ē	bee	s	sauce
f	fife, phase, rough	sh	ship, dish
		t	tight, stopped
g	gag	th	thin
h	hat	*th*	this
hw	which	ŭ	cut
ĭ	pit	ûr	urge, term, firm, word, heard
ī	pie, by		
îr	deer, pier		
j	judge	v	valve
k	kick, cat, pique	w	with
l	lid, needle	y	yes
m	mum	z	zebra, xylem
n	no, sudden	zh	vision, pleasure, garage
ng	thing		
ŏ	pot		
ō	toe	ə	about, item, edible, gallop, circus
ô	caught, paw		
ôr	core	ər	butter

I want to talk a little bit about what conservative leaders need to do—some truths they need to acknowledge. For one, they need to understand the critical role that the separation of church and state has played in preserving not only our democracy, but the robustness of our religious practice. Folks tend to forget that during our founding, it wasn't the atheists or the civil libertarians who were the most effective champions of the First Amendment. It was the persecuted minorities, it was Baptists like John Leland who didn't want the established churches to impose their views on folks who were getting happy out in the fields and teaching the scripture to slaves. It was the forebears of the evangelicals who were the most **adamant** about not mingling government with religious, because they did not want state-sponsored religion hindering their ability to practice their faith as they understood it.

— Barack Obama, keynote address, Call to Renewal conference, June 28, 2006

adamant (ad′ə-mənt)

adjective

Impervious to pleas, appeals, or reason; stubbornly unyielding.

> Henry Ford himself was **adamant** about lean and clean operating policies, saving his company millions of dollars by reducing waste and setting new standards with his time-saving assembly line. "You must get the most out of the power, out of the material, and out of the time," he wrote in 1926, a credo that most contemporary CEOs would proudly hang on their office walls.
>
> —William McDonough and Michael Braungart,
> *Cradle to Cradle: Remaking the Way We Make Things,* 2002

[From Middle English *adamaunt*, diamond, indestructible thing, from Old French, from Latin *adamās, adamant-*, from Greek, hard metal, diamond (literally, unable to be overcome) : *a-*, not + *damān*, to overpower, akin to English *tame.*]

affectation (ăf′ĕk-tā′shən)

noun

1. A mannerism or habit that is assumed rather than natural, especially to impress others. **2.** Behavior characterized by such mannerisms or habits; artificiality.

> This new dialect of England's ruling class differed markedly from the speech ways of American colonists, to whom it seemed contrived and pretentious. . . . Loyalists who fled to Britain after the Revolution were startled to discover that their old-fashioned speech and manners were far removed from the latest **affectations** of London drawing rooms.
>
> — David Hackett Fischer, *Albion's Seed: Four British Folkways in America,* 1989

> To gain the affections of a virtuous man is **affectation** necessary?
>
> — Mary Wollstonecraft, *A Vindication of the Rights of Woman,* 1792

[From Latin *affectātiō, affectātiōn-,* from *affectātus,* past participle of *affectāre,* to strive after, frequentative of *afficere, affect-,* to influence, do to, act on : *ad-,* to, toward + *facere,* to do.]

affinity (ə-fĭn′ĭ-tē)

noun

1. A natural attraction, liking, or feeling of kinship. **2.** An inherent similarity between persons or things.

> I enjoy the unselfconscious moments of a shared cultural intimacy, whatever form they take, when no one else is watching, when no white people are around. . . . Even so, I rebel at the notion that I can't be part of other groups, that I can't construct identities through elective **affinity,** that race must be the most important thing about me.
>
> — Henry Louis Gates, Jr., *Colored People: A Memoir,* 1994

> The superficial religious **affinities** between the Puritan Commonwealth and the Dutch Republic did nothing to palliate the bitter maritime disputes that produced the first Anglo-Dutch war in 1651.
>
> — Simon Schama, *The Embarrassment of Riches: An Interpretation of Dutch Culture in the Golden Age,* 1987

[From Middle English *affinite,* kinship, from Old French *afinite,* relationship by marriage, from Latin *affīnitās,* from *affīnis,* bordering on, neighboring, related by marriage : *ad-,* to, toward + *fīnis,* boundary.]

allay (ə-lā′)

verb

To calm or pacify; set to rest.

> Really it is very painfull to be 400 Miles from ones Family and Friends when We know they are in Affliction. It seems as if It would be a joy to me to fly home, even to share with you your Burdens and Misfortunes. Surely, if I were with you, it would be my Study to **allay** your Griefs, to mitigate your Pains and to divert your melancholly Thoughts.
>
> — John Adams, from a letter to Abigail Adams (in its original spelling), October 19, 1775

[From Middle English *aleien,* from Old English *ālecgan,* to lay down : *ā-*, intensive prefix + *lecgan,* to lay.]

amelioration (ə-mēl′yə-rā′shən)

noun

The act or process of improving something or the state of being improved.

> They gave him their attention, the prime ministers, the archbishops, the princes: they had begun to be gravely alarmed by the unrest of the lower orders. . . . [Robert] Owen was still able to believe in their disinterestedness. It had never occurred to him that for persons like them, in positions of high responsibility, it would be possible to desire anything other than the general **amelioration** of humanity. Then a critical incident occurred which caused him to change his mind.
>
> — Edmund Wilson, *To the Finland Station,* 1940

[Alteration (on the model of French *améliorer*, ameliorate) of earlier *meliorate*, to ameliorate, from Latin *meliōrāre*, *meliōrāt-*, from *melior*, better.]

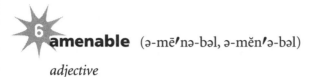

amenable (ə-mē′nə-bəl, ə-měn′ə-bəl)

adjective

1. Responsible to higher authority; accountable. **2.** Susceptible or open, as to testing or criticism. **3.** Responsive to advice, authority, or suggestion; willing.

> The President of the United States would be liable to be impeached, tried, and, upon conviction of treason, bribery, or other high crimes or misdemeanors, removed from office; and would afterwards be liable to prosecution and punishment in the ordinary course of law. The person of the king of Great Britain is sacred and inviolable; there is no constitutional tribunal to which he is **amenable**; no punishment to which he can be subjected without involving the crisis of a national revolution.
>
> — Alexander Hamilton, "Federalist No. 69," March 14, 1788

> Once theology tried to turn itself into science, it could only produce a caricature of rational discourse, because these truths are not **amenable** to scientific demonstration.
>
> — Karen Armstrong, *The Battle for God,* 2000

Thinking about age is thinking about death. Approaching death: how to parse the phrase? Is it approaching me, or am I approaching it? Either way, will we come face to face in ten minutes or ten months or ten years, and what exactly will be the form of our greeting? Which indignities are in store? Once I thought I'd rather die than live with certain physical humiliations; now I'm more **amenable**. I could manage, given the alternative.

> — Lynne Sharon Schwartz, "At a Certain Age,"
> *The Threepenny Review*, 1999

[Alteration (probably on the model of French *amener*, to lead) of Middle English *menable*, from Old French, from *mener*, to lead, from Latin *mināre*, to drive (livestock or pack animals), from *minārī*, to threaten, from *minae*, threats.]

amoral (ā-môr′əl)

adjective

Not admitting of moral distinctions or judgments; neither moral nor immoral.

> What distinguishes markets is exactly that they are **amoral** — that is to say, moral considerations do not find expression in market prices. That is because efficient markets by definition have so many participants that no single one can affect the market price. Even if some participants are held back by moral scruples, others will take their place at only marginally different prices.
>
> — George Soros, "Why the Markets Can't Fix Themselves," *The New Republic,* September 2, 2002

[From *a-*, without, not (from Greek) + *moral* (from Middle English, from Old French, from Latin *mōrālis*, from *mōs, mōr-*, custom, rule, behavior).]

assuage (ə-swāj′)

verb

To make (something burdensome or painful) less intense or severe.

> While most of us think of politics as a Machiavellian drama in which actors make alliances and take practical steps to advance their material interests, the [conservative] backlash is something very different: a crusade in which one's material interests are suspended in favor of vague cultural grievances that are all-important and yet are incapable of ever being **assuaged**.
>
> — Thomas Frank, *What's the Matter with Kansas?*, 2004

[From Middle English *asswagen*, from Old French *assuagier*, from Vulgar Latin **assuāviāre*: Latin *ad-*, to, toward + Latin *suāvis*, sweet, delightful.]

bauble (bô′bəl)

noun

A small, showy ornament of little value; a trinket.

> The poor inhabitants of Cuba and St. Domingo, when they were first discovered by the Spaniards, used to wear little bits of gold as ornaments in their hair and other parts of their dress. They seemed to value them as we would do any little pebbles of somewhat more than ordinary beauty, and to consider them as just worth the picking up, but not worth the refusing to anybody who asked them. They gave them to their new guests at the first request, without seeming to think that they had made them any very valuable present. They were astonished to observe the rage of the Spaniards to obtain them; and had no notion that there could anywhere be a country in which many people had the disposal of so great a superfluity of food, so scanty always among themselves, that for a very small quantity of those glittering **baubles** they would willingly give as much as might maintain a whole family for many years.
>
> — Adam Smith, *An Inquiry into the Nature and Causes of the Wealth of Nations,* 1776

[From Middle English *babel*, from Old French *babel, baubel*, child's toy, perhaps ultimately imitative of the babbling of babies.]

beguile (bĭ-gīl′)

verb

1. To deceive by guile; delude. **2.** To distract the attention of; divert.

> Almost every problem we have can be ascribed to the fact that human beings are utterly **beguiled** by their feelings of separateness. It would seem that a spirituality that undermined such dualism, through the mere contemplation of consciousness, could not help but improve our situation.
>
> — Sam Harris, *The End of Faith: Religion, Terror, and the Future of Reason*, 2004

> I have been shown in the files of the War Department a statement of the Adjutant General of Massachusetts, that you are the mother of five sons who have died gloriously on the field of battle.
>
> I feel how weak and fruitless must be any words of mine which should attempt to **beguile** you from the grief of a loss so overwhelming. But I cannot refrain from tendering to you the consolation that may be found in the thanks of the Republic they died to save. I pray that our Heavenly Father may assuage the anguish of your bereavement, and leave you only the cherished memory of the loved and lost, and the solemn pride that must be yours, to have laid so costly a sacrifice upon the altar of Freedom.
>
> — Abraham Lincoln, from a letter to Mrs. Bixby, November 21, 1864

[From Middle English *bigilen* : *bi-*, all around, thoroughly (from Old English, akin to *bī*, by) + *gilen*, to deceive (from Old French *guiler*, of Germanic origin; akin to English *wile*).]

beset (bĭ-sĕt′)

verb

1. To attack from all sides. **2.** To trouble persistently; harass.

> We've got to follow through on our ideals or we betray something at the heart of who we are. Outside these gates, and even within them, the culture of idealism is under siege, **beset** by materialism and narcissism and all the other "isms" of indifference — and their defense mechanisms: knowingness, the smirk, the joke.
>
> — Bono, commencement address, Harvard University, Cambridge, MA, June 12, 2001

[From Middle English *bisetten,* from Old English *besettan* : *be-*, all around + *settan,* to set.]

bulwark (bŏŏl′wərk, bŏŏl′wôrk′)

noun

1. A wall or embankment raised as a defensive fortification; a rampart. **2.** Something serving as a defense or safeguard.

> We have seen the necessity of the Union, as our **bulwark** against foreign danger, as the conservator of peace among ourselves, as the guardian of our commerce and other common interests, as the only substitute for those military establishments which have subverted the liberties of the Old World, and as the proper antidote for the diseases of faction, which have proved fatal to other popular governments, and of which alarming symptoms have been betrayed by our own.
>
> — James Madison, "Federalist No. 14," November 30, 1787

> History proves that dictatorships do not grow out of strong and successful governments but out of weak and helpless governments. If by democratic methods people get a government strong enough to protect them from fear and starvation, their democracy succeeds, but if they do not, they grow impatient. Therefore, the only sure **bulwark** of continuing liberty is a government strong enough to protect the interests of the people, and a people strong enough and well enough informed to maintain its sovereign control over its government.
>
> — Franklin D. Roosevelt, "On Economic Conditions," Fireside Chat 12, April 14, 1938

[From Middle English *bulwerk,* from Middle Dutch *bolwerk,* from Middle High German *bolwerc*: *bolle,* plank + *werc,* work (from Old High German).]

---

13 busybody (bĭz′ē-bŏd′ē)

noun

A person who meddles or pries into the affairs of others.

> Of all tyrannies a tyranny sincerely exercised for the good of its victims may be the most oppressive. It may be better to live under robber barons than under omnipotent moral **busybodies**. The robber baron's cruelty may sometimes sleep, his cupidity may at some point be satiated; but those who torment us for our own good will torment us without end for they do so with the approval of their own conscience.
>
> — C. S. Lewis, *God in the Dock,* 1970

[From Modern English *busy* (from Middle English *bisi, busi,* from Old English *bysig,* akin to Dutch *bezig*) + *body* (from Middle English *bodi,* from Old English *bodig,* akin to Old High German *botah*).]

complacent (kəm-plā′sənt)

adjective

Contented to a fault; self-satisfied and unconcerned.

> It began to seem that one would have to hold in the mind forever two ideas which seemed to be in opposition. The first idea was acceptance, the acceptance, totally without rancor, of life as it is, and men as they are: in the light of this idea, it goes without saying that injustice is a commonplace. But this did not mean that one could be **complacent**, for the second idea was of equal power: that one must never, in one's own life, accept these injustices as commonplace but must fight them with all one's strength.
>
> — James Baldwin, "Notes of a Native Son," 1955

[From Latin *complacēns, complacent-*, present participle of *complacēre*, to please : *com-*, intensive prefix + *placēre*, to please.]

concomitant (kən-kŏm'ĭ-tənt)

adjective

Occurring or existing concurrently.

> Things happen suddenly in Wyoming, the change of seasons and weather; for people, the violent swings in and out of isolation. But good-naturedness is **concomitant** with severity. Friendliness is a tradition. Strangers passing on the road wave hello. A common sight is two pickups stopped side by side far out on a range, on a dirt track winding through the sage. The drivers will share a cigarette, uncap their thermos bottles, and pass a battered cup, steaming with coffee, between windows.
>
> — Gretel Ehrlich, *The Solace of Open Spaces,* 1985

[From Late Latin *concomitāns, concomitant-,* present participle of *concomitārī,* to accompany : Latin *com-,* with + Latin *comitārī,* to accompany (from *comes, comit-,* companion).]

16 consign (kən-sīn′)

verb

To turn over permanently to another's charge or to a lasting condition; commit irrevocably.

> Great was the agitation in the little community of Palos as they beheld the well-known vessel of the admiral reentering their harbor. Their desponding imaginations had already **consigned** him to a watery grave; for, in addition to the preternatural horrors which hung over the voyage, they had experienced the most stormy and disastrous winter within the recollection of the oldest mariners.
>
> — William Hickling Prescott, "Return of Columbus," *History of the Reign of Ferdinand and Isabella, the Catholic, of Spain,* 1842

> The Conservative knows that to regard man as part of an undifferentiated mass is to **consign** him to ultimate slavery.
>
> — Barry Goldwater, *The Conscience of a Conservative,* 1960

[From Middle English *consignen,* to certify by seal, from Old French *consigner,* from Latin *cōnsignāre* : *com-,* with (also used as an intensive prefix) + *signāre,* to mark (from *signum,* mark).]

contend (kən-tĕnd′)

verb

1. To strive in opposition or against difficulties; struggle. **2.** To maintain or assert.

> His everyday behavior was that of a concerned friend who wanted to help families **contending** with one terrible emergency after another.
>
> — Robert Coles, *The Call of Service: A Witness to Idealism,* 1993

> It is not my contention that chemical insecticides must never be used. I do **contend** that we have put poisonous and biologically potent chemicals indiscriminately into the hands of persons largely or wholly ignorant of their potentials for harm. We have subjected enormous numbers of people to contact with these poisons, without their consent and often without their knowledge. If the Bill of Rights contains no guarantee that a citizen shall be secure against lethal poisons distributed either by private individuals or by public officials, it is surely only because our forefathers, despite their considerable wisdom and foresight, could conceive of no such problem.
>
> — Rachel Carson, *Silent Spring,* 1962

[From Middle English *contenden,* from Latin *contendere* : *com-,* with + *tendere,* to stretch, strive.]

---

cosmopolitan (kŏz′mə-pŏl′ĭ-tn)

adjective

1. Having constituent elements from all over the world or from many different parts of the world. **2.** So sophisticated as to be at home in all parts of the world or conversant with many spheres of interest.

> We do not need, have never needed, settled community, a homogeneous system of values, in order to have a home. Cultural purity is an oxymoron. The odds are that, culturally speaking, you already live a **cosmopolitan** life, enriched by literature, art, and film that come from many places, and that contains influences from many more.
>
> — Kwame Anthony Appiah, *Cosmopolitanism: Ethics in a World of Strangers,* 2006

> [Dwight] Macdonald remained active in Trotskyist circles. . . . He valued Leon Trotsky, above all, as a model of the cultured, **cosmopolitan** intellectual, a man who had achieved the rare combination of radical thinking and effective action.
>
> — Gregory D. Sumner, *Dwight Macdonald and the Politics Circle: The Challenge of Cosmopolitan Democracy,* 1996

[From Modern English *cosmopolite,* cosmopolitan person (from Greek *kosmopolītēs* : *kosmos,* world + *polītēs,* citizen, from *polis,* city) + *-an,* suffix forming adjectives (on the model of *metropolitan*).]

culpable (kŭl′pə-bəl)

adjective

Deserving of blame or censure; blameworthy.

Society is a very **culpable** entity, and has to answer for the manufacture of many unwholesome commodities, from bad pickles to bad poetry.

— George Eliot, "Silly Novels by Lady Novelists," *Westminster Review LXVI,* October 1856

[From Middle English *coupable,* from Old French, from Latin *culpābilis,* from *culpāre,* to blame, from *culpa,* fault.]

Donald killed his girl while under the influence of PCP. He had, or seemed to have, no memory of the deed. . . . The details [of the murder], manifest on forensic examination, were macabre, and could not be revealed in open court. . . . Comparison was made with the acts of violence occasionally committed during temporal lobe or psychomotor seizures. There is no memory of such acts, and perhaps no intention of violence—those who commit them are considered neither responsible nor **culpable**, but are none the less committed for their own and others' safety.

— Oliver Sacks, "Murder,"
*The Man Who Mistook
His Wife for a Hat and
Other Clinical Tales,*
1970

depravity (dĭ-prăv′ĭ-tē)

noun

A morally corrupt act or condition.

> I have been reading the morning paper. I do it every morning — knowing well that I shall find in it the usual **depravities** and basenesses and hypocrisies and cruelties that make up civilization, and cause me to put in the rest of the day pleading for the damnation of the human race. I cannot seem to get my prayers answered, yet I do not despair.
>
> — Mark Twain, from a letter to William Dean Howells, April 2, 1899

[From Modern English *deprave* (from Middle English *depraven,* to corrupt, from Old French *depraver,* from Latin *dēprāvāre* : *dē-,* completely + *prāvus,* crooked) + *-ity,* noun-forming suffix.]

derelict (dĕr′ə-lĭkt′)

adjective

Neglectful of duty or obligation; remiss.

> We call ourselves "public servants" but I'll tell you this:
> We as public servants must set an example for the rest
> of the nation. It is hypocritical for the public official to
> admonish and exhort the people to uphold the common
> good if we are **derelict** in upholding the common good.

> — Barbara Jordan, keynote address, Democratic
> National Convention, 1976

[From Latin *dērelictus*, past participle of *dērelinquere*, to abandon : *dē-*, apart, away, completely + *relinquere*, to leave behind, relinquish (from *re-*, back + *linquere*, to leave).]

dissimulate (dĭ-sĭm′yə-lāt′)

verb

To conceal one's true feelings or intentions.

> However dull or morally delinquent an artist may be, in his moment of creation when his work pierces to the truth, he cannot **dissimulate**, he cannot fake it. Tolstoy once remarked that what we look for in the work of art is the revelation of the artist's soul, a glimpse of god. You can't act that.
>
> — Arthur Miller, "On Politics and the Art of Acting," 30th Jefferson Lecture in the Humanities, Washington, DC, March 26, 2001

[From Middle English *dissimulaten,* from Latin *dissimulāre, dissimulāt-* : *dis-,* apart, asunder + *simulāre, simulāt-,* to simulate (from *similis,* like, similar).]

dissipate (dĭs'ə-pāt')

verb

1. To drive away; disperse. **2.** To spend, use, or engage in intemperately or foolishly.

> I believe it is the duty of every learned person to be a force for expanding endlessly the spirit of openness, love, and acceptance that **dissipates** ill will, finds common ground within difference, and advances cooperation.
>
> — Ruth Simmons, commencement address, The Jewish Theological Seminary, May 20, 2004

> The main of life is, indeed, composed of small incidents, and petty occurrences; of wishes for objects not remote, and grief for disappointments of no fatal consequence; of insect vexations which sting us and fly away, impertinencies which buzz a while about us, and are heard no more; of meteorous pleasures which dance before us and are **dissipated**; of compliments which glide off the soul like other musick, and are forgotten by him that gave and him that received them.
>
> — Samuel Johnson, *The Rambler,* No. 68, November 10, 1750

[From Middle English *dissipaten,* from Latin *dissipāre, dissipāt-,* to dissipate.]

distill also **distil** (dĭ-stĭl′)

verb

1. To increase the concentration of, separate, or purify by heating a mixture and collecting the vapors. **2.** To separate or extract the essence or most important parts of.

> Sunlight may **distil** water from the sea, later to fall as rain on the land, but sunlight does not spontaneously at the Earth's surface split oxygen from water and drive reactions leading to the synthesis of intricate compounds and structures.
>
> — James Lovelock, *Gaia: A New Look at Life on Earth,* 1979

> The CIA had learned years before that Ronald Reagan was not much of a reader. Dense, detailed briefings about global affairs rarely reached his desk. But Reagan loved movies. [CIA director William] Casey encouraged his colleagues to **distill** important intelligence so the president could watch it on a movie screen.
>
> — Steve Coll, *Ghost Wars: The Secret History of the CIA, Afghanistan, and bin Laden, from the Soviet Invasion to September 10, 2001,* 2004

[From Middle English *distillen,* from Old French *distiller,* let fall drop by drop, decant, from Latin *distillāre,* variant of *dēstillāre,* to trickle : *dē-,* down + *stillāre,* to drip (from *stilla,* drop).]

dogmatic (dôg-măt′ĭk)

adjective

1. Of or relating to an authoritative principle, belief, or statement of ideas or opinion, especially a dogma (a doctrine of faith set forth by a church). **2.** Characterized by an authoritative, arrogant assertion of unproved or unprovable principles.

> Even our intellectual life was subject to regulation. Teaching in every subject was **dogmatic**, and there was little chance to raise questions. Dr. Bob's interpretation of doctrine, ethics, and academics was the only one allowed.
>
> — Billy Graham, *Just As I Am: The Autobiography of Billy Graham,* 1997

> When people are least sure they are often most **dogmatic**. We do not know what the Russians intend, so we state with great assurance what they will do. We compensate for our inability to foretell the consequences of, say, rearming Germany by asserting positively just what the consequences will be. So it is in economics.
>
> — John Kenneth Galbraith, *The Great Crash, 1929,* 1954

[From Late Latin *dogmaticus,* from Greek *dogmatikos,* from *dogma, dogmat-,* belief, from *dokein,* to seem, think.]

elicit (ĭ-lĭsʹĭt)

verb

To call forth, draw out, or provoke (a reaction, for example).

> In a way, to be indifferent to that suffering is what makes the human being inhuman. Indifference, after all, is more dangerous than anger and hatred. Anger can at times be creative. One writes a great poem, a great symphony. One does something special for the sake of humanity because one is angry at the injustice that one witnesses. But indifference is never creative. Even hatred at times may **elicit** a response. You fight it. You denounce it. You disarm it.
>
> — Elie Wiesel, "The Perils of Indifference," speech at the White House, Washington, DC, April 12, 1999

[From Latin *ēlicere, ēlicit-* : *ē-, ex-*, out of + *lacere*, to entice.]

epithet (ĕp′ə-thĕt′)

noun

1. A term used to characterize a person or thing, such as *rosy-fingered* in *rosy-fingered dawn* or *the Great* in *Catherine the Great.* **2.** A term used as a descriptive substitute for the name or title of a person, such as *The Great Emancipator* for Abraham Lincoln.

> Children, I grant, should be "innocent"; but when the **epithet** is applied to men, or women, it is but a civil term for weakness.
>
> — Mary Wollstonecraft, *A Vindication of the Rights of Woman,* 1792

> Primordial black holes with initial masses [slightly greater than a thousand million tons] would still be emitting radiation in the form of X rays and gamma rays. . . . Such holes hardly deserve the **epithet** black: they really are white hot and are emitting energy at a rate of about ten thousand megawatts.
>
> — Stephen Hawking, *A Brief History of Time,* 1988

[Latin *epitheton,* from Greek, neuter of *epithetos,* added, attributed, from *epitithenai, epithe-,* to add to : *epi-,* upon ı *tithenai,* to place.]

espouse (ĭ-spouz´)

verb

To support or advocate (a cause, for example).

> Those who **espouse** violence exploit people. To call men to arms with many promises, to ask them to give up their lives for a cause and then not produce for them afterwards, is the most vicious type of oppression.
>
> — César Chávez, "He Showed Us the Way," speech commemorating Martin Luther King, Jr., April 1978

[From Middle English *espousen,* from Old French *espouser,* from Latin *spōnsāre,* to become engaged to (a woman), from *spōnsa,* fiancée, bride, from *spondēre,* to promise, betroth.]

29 expediency (ĭk-spē′dē-ən-sē)

noun

Adherence to practical but convenient or self-serving means.

> When men come up against the inevitable arithmetic of the political situation, that more women in the House and Senate means fewer men, idealism moves over for **expediency**, and we hear talk of a male backlash and audible discontent about so-called quota systems.
>
> — Bella Abzug, "Every Issue Is a Woman's Issue," speech at the Commonwealth Club of California, San Francisco, March 23, 1973

[From Modern English *expedient,* from Middle English *expedient,* conducive to a result, suitable, from Latin *expediēns, expedient-,* present participle of *expedīre,* to set free (as from a snare holding the feet), make ready : *ex-,* out of + *pēs, ped-,* foot.]

forestall (fôr-stôl′)

verb

To delay, hinder, or prevent by taking precautionary measures beforehand.

> Because monetary policy works with a lag, we need to be forward looking, taking actions to **forestall** imbalances that may not be visible for many months. There is no alternative to basing actions on forecasts, at least implicitly.
>
> — Alan Greenspan, "The Challenge of Central Banking in a Democratic Society," Francis Boyer Lecture, American Enterprise Institute for Public Policy Research, Washington, DC, December 5, 1996

[From Middle English *forestallen,* to waylay and rob, from *forestal,* ambush, waylaying, highway robbery, from Old English *foresteall* : *fore-,* in front + *steall,* position.]

Doctors and public health officers, in fact, have probably **forestalled** epidemics that might have checked or even reversed the massive worldwide growth of human population that distinguishes our age from all that have gone before.

— William H. McNeill,
Plagues and Peoples,
1976

furtive (fûr′tĭv)

adjective

Characterized by an attempt to avoid notice, especially out of fear of being caught doing something wrong; stealthy or surreptitious.

> I wish we were a hedonistic culture and saw sexual pleasure as a normal part of civilized life, like tasty meals and summer vacations and opera tickets. But under the Playboy glitz, we're still the same old Puritans who thought Massachusetts winters were good for the soul. We still suspect sex entails punishment — an attitude strongly reinforced by the new sexually transmitted diseases — and because contraception breaks this connection, we can't acknowledge it except in a worried, **furtive** way.
>
> — Katha Pollitt, "Hers," *New York Times,* January 2, 1986

[From French *furtif,* from Old French, from Latin *fūrtīvus,* from *fūrtum,* theft, from *fūr,* thief.]

galling (gô'lĭng)

adjective

Causing extreme irritation or chagrin; vexing.

> Unemployment is one of the bitter and **galling** problems that now afflicts mankind. It has been with us, in a measure, since the beginning of our industrial era. It has been increased by the complexity of business and industry, and it has been made more acute by the Depression.
>
> — Franklin D. Roosevelt, "On the Unemployment Census," Fireside Chat 11, November 14, 1937

[From Middle English *galle*, a skin sore caused by friction and abrasion, from Old English *gealla*, possibly from Latin *galla*, oak gall.]

gloat (glōt)

verb

To feel or express great, often malicious, pleasure or self-satisfaction.

> Should you wish to make sure that your birthday will be celebrated three hundred years hence, your best course is undoubtedly to keep a diary. Only first be certain that you have the courage to lock your genius in a private book and the humour to **gloat** over a fame that will be yours only in the grave. For the good diarist writes either for himself alone or for a posterity so distant that it can safely hear every secret and justly weigh every motive.
>
> — Virginia Woolf, "Rambling Round Evelyn," *The Common Reader,* 1925

[From a source perhaps akin to Old Norse *glotta,* to smile scornfully, and German *glotzen,* to stare.]

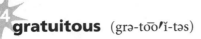

gratuitous (grə-tōō′ĭ-təs)

adjective

Unnecessary or unwarranted; unjustified.

> Positive words become meaningless when offered habitually and excessively. Frequent and **gratuitous** praise removes the great value of a sincere compliment. Leaders who dole it out with little thought sacrifice a most powerful motivational ally — the pat on the back.
>
> — John Wooden and Steve Jamison, *Wooden on Leadership,* 2005

> Social reformers, and educational reformers in particular, often self-righteously take for granted that parents, especially those who are poor and have little education themselves, have little interest in their children's education and no competence to choose for them. That is a **gratuitous** insult. Such parents have frequently had limited opportunity to choose. However, U.S. history has amply demonstrated that, given the opportunity, they have often been willing to sacrifice a great deal, and have done so wisely, for their children's welfare.
>
> — Milton Friedman and Rose Friedman, *Free to Choose: A Personal Statement,* 1980

[From Latin *grātuītus,* done without pay or reward, voluntary, unprovoked, akin to *grātus,* pleasing, deserving thanks, and *grātia,* favor, courtesy.]

hallmark (hôl′märk′)

noun

A conspicuous feature or characteristic, especially a positive one.

> After several weeks of overwork, lost sleep and anxiety she too experienced the painful sore throat, fever and throat-tightening constriction that were the **hallmarks** of diphtheria, and she took to her bed, unable to do any more for her ravaged family.
>
> — Carolly Erickson, *Alexandra: The Last Tsarina*, 2001

[After Goldsmith's Hall in London, England, where gold and silver articles have been appraised and stamped with marks indicating purity since the 1300s.]

If we keep terrorist attacks in perspective and recognize that the strongest weapons in our arsenal against terrorism are precisely the **hallmarks** of democracy that we value, then we can indeed contain the terrorist threat.

— Louise Richardson,
What Terrorists Want,
2006

36 **happenstance** (hăp'ən-stăns')

noun

A chance circumstance.

> It may be a memory lapse, but I don't recall thinking about marriage much at all until I fell in love. I was 29; late, that's agreed. But the point is that for me (and for my generation as a whole, I believe, though you hate to make a statement like that), marriage loomed only as an outgrowth of **happenstance**; you met a person. Today's graduates, however, seem uneasy with that kind of serendipity.
>
> — Bruce Weber, "Alone Together: The Unromantic Generation," *New York Times,* April 5, 1987

[From Modern English *happen* + *(circum)stance.*]

37 **ignominious** (ĭg′nə-mĭn′ē-əs)

adjective

Characterized by or deserving shame or disgrace.

> For Marcos it was an **ignominious** end. He had cringed in his palace for three disastrous days, watching incredulously as a desperate mutiny by a handful of soldiers blossomed into full-scale revolt. His once loyal military turned against him in an avalanche of revulsion; hostile crowds threatened to storm the palace gates. And it was finally left to his old ally Ronald Reagan to inform the fading dictator that he was through.
>
> — Harry Anderson, "Cory's 'People Power,'"
> *Newsweek,* March 10, 1986

[From French *ignominieux,* from Latin *ignōminiōsus,* from *ignōminia,* disgrace, ignominy : *i-, in-,* not + *nōmen,* name, reputation (influenced by *gnōscere,* to know).]

imperturbable (ĭm′pər-tûr′bə-bəl)

adjective

Unshakably calm and collected.

> One night . . . we were discussing with Harry Hooker the question of compulsory military service for all young men as a peacetime measure. . . . I disliked the idea thoroughly and argued against it heatedly. . . . In the end, I evidently made Franklin feel I was really arguing against him and I suddenly realized he was upset. I stopped at once. . . . I knew only too well that in discussing the issue I had forgotten that Franklin was no longer the calm and **imperturbable** person who, in the past, had always goaded me on to vehement arguments when questions of policy came up. It was just another indication of the change which we were all so unwilling to acknowledge.
>
> — Eleanor Roosevelt, *This I Remember,* 1949

[From Middle English, from Old French, from Late Latin *imperturbābilis* : Latin *in-*, not + Latin *perturbāre*, to disturb (from *per-*, thoroughly + *turbāre*, to throw into disorder, from *turba*, confusion, perhaps from Greek *turbē*, confusion).]

---

ingratiate (ĭn-grā′shē-āt′)

verb

To bring (oneself, for example) into the favor or good graces of another, especially by deliberate effort.

> It was useless to hope for a Cabinet post . . . but if he **ingratiated** himself with McKinley now, and worked hard to ensure his election in November, he might count on some fairly high-level job next spring.
>
> — Edmund Morris, *The Rise of Theodore Roosevelt,* 1979

[Perhaps from Italian *ingraziare,* from *in grazia,* into favor, from Latin *in grātiam* : *in,* in + *grātiam,* accusative of *grātia,* favor (from *grātus,* pleasing).]

innocuous (ĭ-nŏk′yōō-əs)

adjective

Having no adverse effect; harmless.

> To my oxygen-depleted mind, the clouds drifting up the grand valley of ice known as the Western Cwm looked **innocuous**, wispy, insubstantial. Gleaming in the brilliant midday sun, they appeared no different from the harmless puffs of convection condensation that rose from the valley almost every afternoon.
>
> — Jon Krakauer, *Into Thin Air: A Personal Account of the Mt. Everest Disaster,* 1997

[From Latin *innocuus*: *in-*, not + *nocuus,* harmful (from *nocēre,* to harm, akin to *nex,* violent death).]

Never before had FBI files been revealed without authorization. The image of a rogue agency manipulating, infiltrating, and interfering not only with militant groups but with mainstream, even **innocuous** organizations like the phone company and the Boy Scouts was given substance by memos and reports that described such tactics in detail. For the first time in its history, the FBI was made to seem to the public at large simultaneously sinister and ridiculous.

— James Carroll, *An American Requiem*, 1996

intemperate (ĭn-tĕm′pər-ĭt, ĭn-tĕm′prĭt)

adjective

Not temperate or moderate; immoderate or excessive.

I regret and yet can understand the somewhat **intemperate** tone of your recent letter. After all we approach the problems confronting us from opposite philosophical points of view.

Is it possible that we have let ideology, political and economical philosophy and governmental policies keep us from considering the very real, everyday problems of the people we represent?

— Ronald Reagan, from a letter to Leonid Brezhnev, April 18, 1981, in *Reagan: A Life in Letters,* edited by Kiron K. Skinner, Annelise Anderson, and Martin Anderson, 2003

[From Middle English *intemperat,* from Latin *intemperātus,* from past participle of *temperāre,* to temper, probably from variant of *tempus, tempor-,* time, season.]

42 interpolate (ĭn-tûr′pə-lāt′)

verb

To insert or introduce between other elements or parts, as in a text or conversation.

> Expository writing requires language to express far more complex trains of thought than it was biologically designed to do. . . . Unlike a conversational partner, a reader will rarely share enough background assumptions to **interpolate** all the missing premises that make language comprehensible. Overcoming one's natural egocentrism and trying to anticipate the knowledge state of a generic reader at every stage of the exposition is one of the most important tasks in writing well.
>
> — Steven Pinker, *The Language Instinct: How the Mind Creates Language,* 1994

[From Latin *interpolāre, interpolāt-,* to touch up, refurbish, from *interpolis,* refurbished : *inter-,* between + *polīre,* to polish.]

inure (ĭn-yŏŏr′)

verb

To habituate a person to something undesirable, especially by prolonged subjection; accustom.

> I hope by degrees we shall be **inured** to hardships and become a virtuous valient people, forgetting our formour Luxery and each one apply with industery and frugality to Manufactory and husbandery till we rival all other Nations by our Virtues.
>
> — Abigail Adams, from a letter to John Adams (in its original spelling), October 21, 1775

> Second-stage weapons, Oppenheimer went on — meaning presumably advanced fission weapons with improved implosion systems — might be equal to 50,000 to 100,000 tons of TNT. Thermonuclear weapons might range from 10 million to 100 million tons TNT equivalent. These were numbers most of the men in the room had seen before and were **inured** to. Apparently Byrnes had not; they worried him gravely.
>
> — Richard Rhodes, *The Making of the Atomic Bomb,* 1986

[Back-formation from Middle English *enured,* customary, from *in ure,* in conformity with custom, in the habit of, in use : *in,* in + *ure,* custom, habit (from Old French *euvre, uevre,* work, from Latin *opera*).]

jingoism (jĭng′gō-ĭz′əm)

noun

Extreme nationalism characterized especially by a belligerent foreign policy; chauvinistic patriotism.

> Greek history is a panorama of **jingoism** and imperialism — war for war's sake, all the citizens being warriors. It is horrible reading — because of the irrationality of it all — save for the purpose of making "history" — and the history is that of the utter ruin of a civilization in intellectual respects perhaps the highest the earth has ever seen.
>
> — William James, "The Moral Equivalent of War," 1910

[From Modern English *jingo*, Chauvinistic patriot (from the phrase *by jingo*, used in the refrain of a bellicose 19th-century English music-hall song, from alteration of *by Jesus*) + *-ism.*]

45

juggernaut (jŭg′ər-nôt′)

noun

An overwhelming or unstoppable force.

The Computer Revolution offers wondrous new possibilities for creative destruction. One goal of capitalist creativity is the globalized economy. One — unplanned — candidate for capitalist destruction is the nation-state, the traditional site of democracy. The computer turns the untrammeled market into a global **juggernaut** crashing across frontiers, enfeebling national powers of taxation and regulation, undercutting national management of interest rates and exchange rates, widening disparities of wealth both within and between nations, dragging down labor standards, degrading the environment, denying nations the shaping of their own economic destiny, accountable to no one, creating a world economy without a world polity. Cyberspace is beyond national control.

— Arthur Schlesinger, Jr., "Has Democracy a Future?" *Foreign Affairs,* September / October, 1997

Names weren't always subject to fashion. About half of all boys in Raleigh Colony were named John, Thomas or William, and more than half of newborn girls in the Massachusetts Bay Colony were named Mary, Elizabeth or Sarah. Even in the 20th century, John, William, James and Robert were, in some combination, the top three names for boys for more than 50 years. Among girls, Mary held on to No. 1 for 46 years, when it was supplanted for six years by Linda, fought its way back for another nine, then succumbed to the **juggernaut** of Lisa.

— Peggy Orenstein, "Where Have All the Lisas Gone?" *New York Times,* July 6, 2003

[From Hindi *jagannāth,* title of Krishna, from Sanskrit *ja-gannāthaḥ,* lord of the world : *jagat,* moving, animate being, the world (from earlier present participle of *jigāti,* he goes) + *nāthaḥ,* lord (from *nāthate,* he helps, protects).]

𝜞𝔞 *WORD HISTORY:* For centuries, the city of Puri in eastern India has held an annual festival in honor of the god Krishna, worshipped under his Sankrit title *Jagannāthaḥ,* "Lord of the World." During the middle of the rainy season, in June and July, devotees help transport Krishna, his brother Baladeva, and his sister Subhadra from the huge bustling temple where they usually reside to another temple some two and a half miles away. There, Krishna and his family enjoy the fresh greenery of the rainy season until they return to their home after a week or two. The objects representing Krishna and his siblings are transported in three chariots—massive towerlike structures about 45 feet high, mounted on wheels, lavishly decorated, and draped with bright cloth. The chariots are drawn with ropes by thousands of devotees, and a huge crowd of over a million pilgrims cheers them on. Worshippers try to touch the ropes, thought to confer blessings. Some have been crushed in the throng or have fallen under the wheels, and on occasion, people desiring release from painful illness have thrown themselves in the chariots' path. Early Western observers in colonial India greatly exaggerated the number of these deaths, however, and sensationalistic reports overshadowed the fact that the festival honors the benevolent god Krishna on the occasion of his pleasure trip. In this way *Jagannāthaḥ* eventually entered English as *juggernaut,* a word for an irresistible force that rolls unstoppably over its victims.

When this creature [the blue whale] is born it is twenty feet long and weighs four tons. . . . It is waaaaay bigger than your car. It drinks a hundred gallons of milk from its mama every day and gains two hundred pounds a day, and when it is seven or eight years old it endures an unimaginable puberty and then it essentially disappears from human **ken**, for next to nothing is known of the mating habits, travel patterns, diet, social life, language, social structure, diseases, spirituality, wars, stories, despairs, and arts of the blue whale. There are perhaps ten thousand blue whales in the world, living in every ocean on earth, and of the largest mammal who ever lived we know nearly nothing. But we know this: the animals with the largest hearts in the world generally travel in pairs, and their penetrating moaning cries, their piercing yearning tongue, can be heard underwater for miles and miles.

— Brian Doyle, "Joyas Voladoras," *The American Scholar,* 2004

ken (kĕn)

noun

Perception; understanding.

> The present moment seems pregnant with great events; but, as you observe, it is beyond the **ken** of mortal foresight to determine what will be the result of those changes which are either making or contemplated in the general system of Europe.
>
> — George Washington, from a letter to
> Gouverneur Morris, July 28, 1791

[From Middle English *kennen,* to know, recognize (influenced by Old Norse *kenna,* to know), from Old English *cennan,* to make known, declare, akin to Old English *cnāwan,* to know.]

latent (lāt′nt)

adjective

Present or potential but not evident or active.

> Yes, you who are reading these lines possess powers of various sorts which you habitually fail to use; and one of these powers you are probably not using to the fullest extent is your magic ability to praise people and inspire them with a realization of their **latent** possibilities. Abilities wither under criticism; they blossom under encouragement.
>
> — Dale Carnegie, *How to Win Friends and Influence People,* 1936

[From Middle English, from Old French, from Latin *latēns, latent-*, present participle of *latēre,* to lie hidden.]

Like children, most small dogs beg to be loved and allowed to love; but Stickeen seemed a very Diogenes, asking only to be let alone: a true child of the wilderness. . . . I was accustomed to look into the faces of plants and animals, and I watched the little sphinx more and more keenly as an interesting study. But there is no estimating the wit and wisdom concealed and latent in our lower fellow mortals until made manifest by profound experiences; for it is through suffering that dogs as well as saints are developed and made perfect.

— John Muir, *Stickeen,*
1909

48 legacy (lĕg′ə-sē)

noun

1. Money or property bequeathed to another by will. **2.** Something handed down from an ancestor or a predecessor or from the past.

> There are said to be around 110 million mines lurking somewhere in the world — and over a third of them are to be found in Africa! . . . Even if the world decided tomorrow to ban these weapons, this terrible **legacy** of mines already in the earth would continue to plague the poor nations of the Globe.
>
> — Diana, Princess of Wales, "Responding to Landmines: A Modern Tragedy and Its Solutions," keynote address, Landmine Survivors Network conference, June 12, 1997

[From Middle English *legacie*, office of a deputy, from Old French, from Medieval Latin *lēgātia*, from Latin *lēgātus*, past participle of *lēgāre*, to depute, bequeath.]

ludicrous (lōō′dĭ-krəs)

adjective

Laughable or hilarious because of obvious absurdity or incongruity.

As late as the spring of 1945, it was possible for one man, with a rifle, to make a difference, however infinitesimal, in the struggle to defeat an enemy who had attacked us and threatened our West Coast. The bomb dropped on Hiroshima made that man **ludicrous**, even pitiful. Soldiering has been relegated to Sartre's theater of the absurd.

— William Manchester, "Okinawa: The Bloodiest Battle of All," *New York Times,* June 14, 1987

[From Latin *lūdicrus,* sportive, from *lūdus,* game.]

mandate (măn′dāt′)

noun

A command or an authorization given by a political electorate to its representative.

> It is for the press to keep the ideals of liberty alive, to ensure that public figures carry out their **mandate**. . . . The press must be used as a mirror from which public figures can see whether they are on the right track.
>
> — Nelson Mandela, speech before the National
> Press Club, October 7, 1994

[From Latin *mandātum*, from neuter past participle of *mandāre*, to command : *manus*, hand + *-dere*, to put (as in *condere*, to put together, establish), from the notion of putting a task in a person's hands.]

maven (mā′vən)

noun

A person who has special knowledge or experience; an expert.

> Science is thus not just a profession. Nor is it a delectation of **mavens**. Nor is it a philosophy. It is a combination of mental operations that has increasingly become the habit of educated peoples.
>
> — Edward O. Wilson, "Science and Ideology," keynote address, convention of the National Association of Scholars, Cambridge, MA, November 1994

[From Yiddish *meyvn*, from Hebrew *mēbîn*, understanding, participle of *hēbîn*, to understand, derived stem of *bîn*, to discern, akin to Arabic *bāna*, to be evident.]

mawkish (mô′kĭsh)

adjective

Excessively and objectionably sentimental.

> I spoke publicly about my sister's death for the very first time when I accepted the Democratic nomination for vice president in 1996, and was surprised that some felt the remarks were **mawkish**.
>
> — Al Gore, *An Inconvenient Truth: The Planetary Emergency of Global Warming and What We Can Do About It*, 2006

[From obsolete and dialectal *mawk*, maggot (from Middle English *mawke*, probably from Old Norse *madhkr*, akin to Modern English *maggot*, alteration of Middle English *maddock*) + *-ish*, suffix forming adjectives.]

"Honesty is the best policy" turns out to be a wise maxim rather than a **mawk-ish** platitude, but only if others follow the same principle. Social trust is a valuable community asset if — but only if — it is warranted.

— Robert D. Putnam,
Bowling Alone: The Collapse and Revival of American Community, 2000

53 modus operandi (mō′dəs ŏp′ə-răn′dē,
 mō′dəs ŏp′ə-răn′dī′)

noun

Plural: **modi operandi** (mō′dē ŏp′ə-răn′dē,
 mō′dī ŏp′ə-răn′dī′)

A method of operating or functioning.

All over the world, recrimination, finger-pointing and par-
tisan condemnation are the **modus operandi** of the new
political order.

> — Benazir Bhutto, speech at the John F. Kennedy
> School of Government, Harvard University,
> Cambridge, MA, November 7, 1997

[From New Latin *modus operandī* : Latin *modus,* mode +
Latin *operandī,* of working, genitive singular of the gerund of
operārī, to work.]

nefarious (nə-fâr′ē-əs)

adjective

Infamous by way of being extremely wicked.

> On escaping into Massachusetts, I went to work on the quays, rolling oil casks, to get a livelihood, and in about three years after having been induced to attend an anti-slavery meeting at Nantucket, it was there announced that I should go from town to town to expose their **nefarious** system. For four years I was then engaged in discussing the slavery question, and during that time I had opportunities of arranging my thoughts and language.
>
> — Frederick Douglass, "I Am Here to Spread Light on American Slavery," speech in Cork, Ireland, October 14, 1845

> The billions of dollars in the Cayman Islands and other such centers are not there because those islands provide better banking services than Wall Street, London, or Frankfurt; they are there because the secrecy allows them to engage in tax evasion, money laundering, and other **nefarious** activities. Only after September 11 was it recognized that among those other **nefarious** activities was the financing of terrorism.
>
> — Joseph E. Stiglitz, *Globalization and Its Discontents,* 2003

[From Latin *nefārius,* from *nefās,* crime, transgression : *ne-,* not + *fās,* divine law.]

nicety (nī′sĭ-tē)

noun

1. The quality of showing or requiring careful, precise treatment; accuracy or precision. **2.** A fine point, small detail, or subtle distinction.

> I supposed him [Samuel Johnson] to be only near-sighted; and indeed I must observe, that in no other respect could I discern any defect in his vision; on the contrary, the force of his attention and perceptive quickness made him see and distinguish all manner of objects, whether of nature or of art, with a **nicety** that is rarely to be found.
>
> — James Boswell, *The Life of Samuel Johnson,* 1791

> Beyond sheer verbal volume, the punch so evident in the Adams prose reflected his more aggressive and confrontational temperament. The Jefferson style was fluid, lyrical, cadenced, and melodious. Words for him were like calming breezes that floated across the pages. The Adams style was excited, jumpy, exclamatory, naughty. Words for him were like weapons designed to pierce the pages or explode above them in illuminating airbursts. While the Adams style generated a host of memorable epigrammatic flashes, it was the worst-possible vehicle for sustaining the diplomatic **niceties**.
>
> — Joseph J. Ellis, *Founding Brothers: The Revolutionary Generation,* 2000

[From Middle English *nicete,* silliness, exactitude, from Old French *nicete,* silliness, from *nice,* silly, from Latin *nescius,* ignorant, from *nescīre,* to be ignorant : *ne-,* not + *scīre,* to know.]

⅋ WORD HISTORY: From a historical perspective, *nicety* looks like it should be the noun corresponding to the adjective *nice*. How is it then that *nicety* means nothing like "kind disposition," or "excellence," since *nice* so often means "kind" or "fine"? As it happens, the meaning of the adjective *nice* has undergone a great deal of change in the past few centuries, while the noun *nicety* has kept pretty much the same meaning it has had since Middle English times.

The story of *nice* begins with the Latin word *nescius*, "ignorant." As Latin developed into Old French, *nescius* developed into *nice*, whose original meaning in Old French was "foolish, without sense." The Old French word was then borrowed into Middle English. By the 15th century, English *nice* had acquired the sense "overrefined," especially in conduct and dress — that is, "elegant to the point of foolishness." From there, *nice* developed senses like "fastidious," "precise," and "subtle." *Nice* is still used in such senses today, in phrases like *a nice distinction*. *Nicety* is the noun corresponding to these senses of *nice*. However, in the 18th century, *nice* the adjective began to be used as a vague term of approval, as in *a nice walk*, but the noun *nicety* did not follow suit.

At the time, some commentators on the language thought that in the case of *nice*, linguistic change had gone too far, and *nice* had developed senses that fastidious speakers of English should reject. Samuel Johnson, the great English author who wrote an influential English dictionary published in 1755, disapproved of the vaguely positive *nice* (just as he disapproved of the word *fun*). *Nice* continued to pose usage problems even in 1817, the date of Jane Austen's novel *Northanger Abbey*. Characters in Austen's novel debate the acceptability of the word *nice* after one of them, Catherine, has used it with the meaning "fine" or "great." Eventually, Catherine is led to exclaim: *"I am sure . . . I did not mean to say anything wrong; but it is a nice book, and why should not I call it so?"* English usage eventually took her side in the argument.

nonchalance (nŏn′shə-läns′)

noun

Casual lack of concern.

> **Nonchalance** about health and well-being is what gives smoking its charm. That same nonchalance is at the heart of all really good manners. The most fundamental lesson of etiquette is "be unconcerned." Proper behavior means always giving the appearance of unperturbed grace.
>
> — P. J. O'Rourke, *Modern Manners: An Etiquette Guide for Rude People,* 1989

[From French, from Old French *nonchalant,* present participle of *nonchaloir,* to have no concern for, scorn : *non-,* not + *chaloir,* to cause concern to (from Latin *calēre,* to be warm).]

obdurate (ŏb′dōō-rĭt)

adjective

1. Hardened in wrongdoing or wickedness; stubbornly impenitent. **2.** Not giving in to or altered by persuasion; intractable.

> In relations between individuals, if you ask another person for forgiveness you may be spurned; the one you have injured may refuse to forgive you. The risk is even greater if you are the injured party, wanting to offer forgiveness. The culprit may be arrogant, **obdurate**, or blind; not ready or willing to apologize or to ask for forgiveness.
>
> — Desmond Tutu, *No Future Without Forgiveness*, 1999

> What eventually turned the president against his commanding general was Hooker's **obdurate** failure to follow directions. The general refused to recognize that Lincoln's homespun suggestions were, in fact, commands.
>
> — David Herbert Donald, *Lincoln*, 1995

[From Middle English *obdurat*, from Late Latin *obdūrātus*, past participle of *obdūrāre*, to harden, from Latin, to be persistent, endure : *ob-*, intensive prefix + *dūrus*, hard.]

orthodoxy   (ôr′thə-dŏk′sē)

noun

The quality or state of adhering to what is commonly accepted, customary, or traditional, especially in religion.

> You have made yourself the Trustee for those in every country who seek to mend the evils of our condition by reasoned experiment within the framework of the existing social system. If you fail, rational change will be gravely prejudiced throughout the world, leaving **orthodoxy** and revolution to fight it out. But if you succeed, new and bolder methods will be tried everywhere, and we may date the first chapter of a new economic era from your accession to office.
>
> — John Maynard Keynes, "An Open Letter to President Roosevelt," *New York Times*, December 31, 1933

[From Late Latin *orthodoxia*, from Greek *orthodoxiā* : Greek *orthos*, straight, correct + Greek *doxa*, opinion (from *dokein*, to think) + Greek *-iā*, suffix forming abstract nouns.]

palliate (păl′ē-āt′)

verb

1. To make less severe or intense; mitigate. **2.** To relieve the symptoms of a disease or disorder. **3.** To make (an offense or crime) seem less serious; extenuate.

> Writing, at its best, is a lonely life. Organizations for writers **palliate** the writer's loneliness but I doubt if they improve his writing. He grows in public stature as he sheds his loneliness and often his work deteriorates. For he does his work alone and if he is a good enough writer he must face eternity, or the lack of it, each day.
>
> — Ernest Hemingway, Nobel Prize acceptance speech, 1954

> [Stonewall] Jackson constantly sucked lemons to **palliate** his dyspepsia and refused to season his food with pepper because (he said) it made his left leg ache.
>
> — James M. McPherson, *Battle Cry of Freedom: The Civil War Era,* 1988

> His [Walpole's] well-known financial ability made men turn to him in the hour of distress, as of all statesmen the most fitted to **palliate** it.
>
> — William E. H. Lecky, *A History of England in the Eighteenth Century,* 1878

[From Middle English *palliaten,* from Late Latin *palliāre, palliāt-,* to cloak, palliate, from Latin *pallium,* cloak.]

patina (păt′n-ə, pə-tē′nə)

noun

1. A thin greenish layer, usually basic copper sulfate, that forms on copper or copper alloys, such as bronze, as a result of corrosion. **2.** A change in appearance produced by long-standing behavior, practice, or use.

> Like geography and history, the arts confer a **patina** on the natural world. A vacant stretch of grass becomes humanly important when one reads the sign "Gettysburg." Over the grass hangs an extended canopy of meaning — struggle, corpses, tears, glory — shadowed by a canopy of American words and works, from the Gettysburg Address to the [Robert Gould] Shaw Memorial.
>
> — Helen Vendler, "The Ocean, the Bird, and the Scholar," 33rd Jefferson Lecture in the Humanities, Washington, DC, May 6, 2004

[From Italian *patina*, from Latin *patina*, plate, pan (from the incrustation on ancient metal plates and dishes), from Greek *patanē*, platter.]

penury (pĕn′yə-rē)

noun

Extreme want or poverty; destitution.

> The United Nations too can also play a much bigger part in forcing attention on these broader concerns, if it is liberated from the **penury** in which it has been typically kept by inadequate financial provisions and by the refusal of some member countries to pay their dues.
>
> — Amartya Sen, "Global Doubts as Global Solutions," Alfred Deakin Lecture, Melbourne, Australia, May 15, 2001

[From Middle English *penurie*, from Latin *pēnūria*, scarcity, dearth.]

pernicious (pər-nĭsh′əs)

adjective

Causing great harm; destructive.

> I am persuaded that the world has been tricked into adopting some false and most **pernicious** notions about consistency — and to such a degree that the average man has turned the rights and wrongs of things entirely around and is proud to be "consistent," unchanging, immovable, fossilized, where it should be his humiliation.
>
> — Mark Twain, "Consistency" speech, 1887

[From Middle English *pernicious*, from Old French *pernicios*, from Latin *perniciōsus*, from *perniciēs*, destruction : *per-*, thoroughly + *nex, nec-*, violent death (akin to *nocere*, to harm).]

63 perpetuate (pər-pĕch′ōō-āt′)

verb

To cause to continue indefinitely; make perpetual.

> The argument that this amendment will not solve the problem of sex discrimination is not relevant. If the argument were used against a civil rights bill, as it has been used in the past, the prejudice that lies behind it would be embarrassing. Of course laws will not eliminate prejudice from the hearts of human beings. But that is no reason to allow prejudice to continue to be enshrined in our laws — to **perpetuate** injustice through inaction.
>
> — Shirley Chisholm, "For the Equal Rights Amendment," speech before the US House of Representatives, Washington, DC, August 10, 1970

[From Latin *perpetuāre*, *perpetuāt-*, from *perpetuus*, continuous : *per-*, thoroughly + *petere*, to go toward.]

pittance (pĭt′ns)

noun

A meager monetary allowance, wage, or remuneration.

> It is time to look forward to the day when the farmworker can share in the fruits of his labors. Today, for the sweat off his brow that he leaves in the rich and abundant fields and orchards which he harvests he receives for his part a **pittance**, a pat on the back, and a passport to nowhere. Justice, decency, and humanity demand that progress not pass him over for yet another generation.
>
> — Henry B. González, *Congressional Record,* 89th Congress, 1st Session, Volume 111, Part 5, US Government Printing Office, April 5, 1965

[From Middle English *pitance,* from Old French *pitance,* allowance of food to a monk or poor person, from Medieval Latin *pietantia,* from **pietāns,* **pietant-,* present participle of **pietāre,* to show compassion, from Latin *pietās,* piety, from *pius,* dutiful.]

On the first day of school when I was a kid, the guy teaching history — and it was almost always a guy, wearing a lot of brown — would cough up the **pompous** same old same old about how if we kids failed to learn the lessons of history then we would be doomed to repeat them. Which is true if you're one of the people who grow up to run things, but not as practical if your destiny is a nice small life.

— Sarah Vowell, *The Partly Cloudy Patriot,* 2002

pompous (pŏm′pəs)

adjective

Characterized by excessive self-esteem or exaggerated dignity; pretentious.

> "The U.S. vs. John Lennon" . . . makes the case that, in just about every way that counted, Lennon was a better person than Richard M. Nixon. That very few people are likely to need persuading on this point is something of a problem. Lennon's status as one of the most beloved popular musicians of recent memory, and one of the best-known cultural figures of the past half-century, leaves the movie with little to do but add its sometimes sanctimonious voice to the chorus of praise and admiration. Luckily, even 26 years after his death, Lennon is a lively enough presence to keep the sentimentality somewhat in check. A great songwriter and a nimble exploiter of his own celebrity, he was also a pretty terrific television talk show guest: witty, engaged and passionate about his beliefs without being **pompous** about it.
>
> — A. O. Scott, "Lennon as Superior to Nixon," *New York Times,* September 15, 2006

[From Middle English *pompous,* from Old French *pompeux,* from Late Latin *pompōsus,* from Latin *pompa,* pomp, procession, from Greek *pompē,* procession, from *pempein,* to send.]

precipitate (prĭ-sĭp′ĭ-tāt′)

verb

To cause to happen, especially suddenly or prematurely.

> In my more than eighteen years at the Federal Reserve, much has surprised me, but nothing more than the remarkable ability of our economy to absorb and recover from the shocks of stock market crashes, credit crunches, terrorism, and hurricanes — blows that would have almost certainly **precipitated** deep recessions in decades past.
>
> — Alan Greenspan, "Economic Flexibility," speech before the Italian American Foundation, Washington, DC, October 12, 2005

[From Latin *praecipitāre, praecipitāt-*, to throw headlong, from *praeceps, praecipit-*, headlong : *prae-*, before + *caput, capit-*, head.]

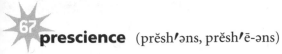

prescience (prĕsh′əns, prĕsh′ē-əns)

noun

Knowledge of actions or events before they occur; foresight.

> There is no doubt that the President foresaw the great dangers closing in upon the pre-war world with far more **prescience** than most well-informed people on either side of the Atlantic, and that he urged forward with all his power such precautionary military preparations as peace-time opinion in the United States could be brought to accept.
>
> — Winston Churchill, "The Greatest Champion of Freedom," eulogy for Franklin D. Roosevelt delivered to the House of Commons, April 17, 1945

[From Middle English *prescience*, from Old French *prescience*, from Late Latin *praescientia*, foreknowledge, from Latin *praesciēns*, *praescient-*, present participle of *praescīre*, to know beforehand : *prae-*, before + *scīre*, to know.]

68 profusion (prə-fyōō'zhən)

noun

An abundant outpouring or quantity.

> When the Kiowas came to the land of the Crows, they could see the dark lees of the hills at dawn across the Bighorn River, the **profusion** of light on the grain shelves, the oldest deity ranging after the solstices. Not yet would they veer southward to the caldron of the land that lay below; they must wean their blood from the northern winter and hold the mountains a while longer in their view.

> — N. Scott Momaday, *The Way to Rainy Mountain*, 1967

[From French *profusion*, from Latin *profūsiō, profūsiōn-*, a pouring out, from *profundere*, to pour forth : *pro-*, forth + *fundere*, to pour.]

69 propensity (prə-pĕn'sĭ-tē)

noun

A natural or innate inclination; a tendency.

Oil companies were becoming marketers, for the first time selling automotive fuel at retail, directly to motorists, at the brand-name stations that were springing up all across the American landscape. Oil wars were not only being fought for supply and markets in foreign lands, but were also erupting in an equally fierce struggle for markets on the main streets of America. And, in its efforts to court consumers, as well as in its inherent **propensity** toward consolidation and integration, the American oil industry began to take on its modern and familiar outline.

— Daniel Yergin, *The Prize: The Epic Quest for Oil, Money, and Power,* 1991

[From archaic Modern English *propense,* inclined, willing, from Latin *prōpēnsus,* past participle of *prōpendēre,* to be inclined : *prō-,* forward + *pendēre,* to hang.]

Lanrezac's staff was urging him to permit a counterattack. . . . Lanrezac refused. He remained silent, gave no orders, waited. . . . To some he appeared **pusillanimous** or paralyzed, to others as a man soberly measuring the chances in an obscure and perilous situation.

— Barbara W. Tuchman,
The Guns of August,
1962

pugnacity (pŭg-năs′ĭ-tē)

noun

A combative or warlike attitude, nature, or inclination; belligerence.

> Modern war is so expensive that we feel trade to be a better avenue to plunder; but modern man inherits all the innate **pugnacity** and all the love of glory of his ancestors. Showing war's irrationality and horror is of no effect upon him. The horrors make the fascination. War is the *strong* life; it is life *in extremis;* war-taxes are the only ones men never hesitate to pay, as the budgets of all nations show us. History is a bath of blood.
>
> — William James, "The Moral Equivalent of War," 1910

[From Latin *pugnācitās*, from *pugnāx, pugnāc-*, combative, from *pugnāre*, to fight, from *pugnus*, fist.]

pusillanimous (pyōo′sə-lăn′ə-məs)

adjective

Lacking courage; cowardly.

> Let any woman who is disquieted by reports of her husband's derelictions figure to herself how long it would have taken him to propose to her if left to his own enterprise, and then let her ask herself if so **pusillanimous** a creature could be imaged in the role of Don Giovanni.
>
> — H. L. Mencken, "A Mythical Dare-Devil," *In Defense of Women,* 1918

[From Middle English *pusillanimus*, from Late Latin *pusillanimis* : Latin *pusillus*, weak (diminutive of *pullus*, young of an animal) + *animus*, mind, spirit, courage.]

quip (kwĭp)

noun

A clever, witty, or sarcastic remark.

verb

To make quips or a quip.

> That he should be guilty of so cheap a **quip** in the midst of a serious discussion, astounded me.
>
> — Jack London, "The Eternity of Forms," *The Turtles of Tasman,* 1916

> Whether Benjamin Franklin **quipped** "We must all hang together, or most assuredly we shall hang separately," is impossible to know, just as there is no way to confirm the much-repeated story that the diminutive John Hancock wrote his name large so the King might read it without his spectacles. But the stories endured because they were in character.
>
> — David McCullough, *John Adams,* 2001

[Alteration of obsolete *quippy,* quip, perhaps from Latin *quippe,* indeed, forsooth (from the use of the interjection in sarcastic remarks).]

Admiration for the quickness of a spoken **quip** somewhat mitigates its cruelty. The exuberance of the retailer of verbal gossip eliminates the implication of scandal, but both quip and gossip become deadly poison when transferred permanently to paper.

— Emily Post, *Etiquette*, 1922

rankle (răng′kəl)

verb

To feel or express irritation or resentment.

> An individual seeking revenge and identifying with oth-
> ers does not become a terrorist in a vacuum. For some-
> one who **rankles** at injustice, identifies with the disad-
> vantaged, and wants to help them, becoming a social
> worker is a more typical career path.
> — Louise Richardson, *What Terrorists Want,* 2006

[From Middle English *ranclen,* fester, from Old French *ran-
cler,* alteration of *draoncler,* from *draoncle,* festering sore,
from Latin *dracunculus,* festering sore (literally, little
dragon), diminutive of *dracō, dracōn-,* serpent, dragon, from
Greek *drakōn.*]

74 reconciliation (rĕk′ən-sĭl′ē-ā′shən)

noun

The reestablishment of a close relationship between individuals or groups.

> We must not use violence. Oh, sometimes as we struggle it will be necessary to boycott. But let us remember as we boycott that a boycott is never an end. A boycott is merely means to awaken within the oppressor the sense of shame and to let him know that we don't like how we are being treated; but the end my friends is **reconciliation**, the end is redemption.
>
> — Martin Luther King, Jr., "A Realistic Look at the Question of Progress in the Area of Race Relations," speech in St. Louis, Missouri, April 10, 1957

[From Middle English *reconsiliacion*, from Old French *reconciliation*, from Latin *reconciliātiō, reconciliātiōn-*, from *reconciliātus*, past participle of *reconciliāre*, to reconcile : *re-*, again + *conciliāre, conciliāt-*, to conciliate (from *concilium*, a calling together, meeting : *com-, con-*, together + *calāre*, to announce, summon).]

resiliency (rĭ-zĭl′yən-sē)

noun

The ability to recover quickly from illness, change, or misfortune.

> But through lack of foresight and constructive imagination the financial and political authorities of the world have lacked the courage or the conviction at each stage of the decline to apply the available remedies in sufficiently drastic doses; and by now they have allowed the collapse to reach a point where the whole system may have lost its **resiliency** and its capacity for a rebound.
>
> — John Maynard Keynes, "The World's Economic Outlook," *The Atlantic Monthly,* May 1932

[From Latin *resiliēns, resilient-*, resilient, present participle of *resilīre*, to leap back : *re-*, back + *salīre*, to leap.]

respite (rĕs′pĭt)

noun

A usually short interval of rest or relief.

> But after a half-century of the Russians are coming, followed by terrorists from proliferating rogue states as well as the ongoing horrors of drug-related crime, there is little **respite** for a people so routinely — so fiercely — disinformed.
>
> — Gore Vidal, "The Meaning of Timothy McVeigh," *Vanity Fair*, September 2001

[From Middle English *respit*, delay, extension (as one granted to a debtor), from Old French *respit*, from Latin *respectus*, looking back, consideration, from past participle of *respicere*, to look back, show concern for : *re-*, back + *specere*, to see, observe.]

 **riposte** (rĭ-pōst′)

noun

1. A quick thrust given after parrying an opponent's lunge in fencing. **2.** A retaliatory action, maneuver, or retort.

> When I see flags sprouting on official lapels, I think of the time in China when I saw Mao's Little Red Book on every official's desk, omnipresent and unread.
>
> But more galling than anything are all those moralistic ideologues in Washington sporting the flag in their lapels while writing books and running Web sites and publishing magazines attacking dissenters as un-American. They are people whose ardor for war grows disproportionately to their distance from the fighting. . . .
>
> So I put this [an American flag lapel pin] on as a modest **riposte** to men with flags in their lapels who shoot missiles from the safety of Washington think tanks, or argue that sacrifice is good as long as they don't have to make it.
>
> — Bill Moyers, from the TV show *NOW with Bill Moyers,* February 28, 2003

[From French, alteration of obsolete *risposte,* from Italian *risposta,* answer, from feminine past participle of *rispondere,* to answer, from Latin *respondēre* : *re-,* back + *spondēre,* to promise.]

sacrosanct (săk′rō-săngkt′)

adjective

Regarded as sacred and inviolable.

> It was the intention of the Revolutionists to establish a system of common education, which should make the teaching of history one of its principal branches; not with the intent of burdening the memories of our youth with the dates of battles or the speeches of generals, nor to make of the Boston Tea Party Indians the one **sacrosanct** mob in all history, to be revered but never on any account to be imitated, but with the intent that every American should know to what conditions the masses of people had been brought by the operation of certain institutions, by what means they had wrung out their liberties, and how those liberties had again and again been filched from them by the use of governmental force, fraud, and privilege.
>
> — Voltairine de Cleyre, *Anarchism and American Traditions*, 1932

[Latin *sacrōsānctus*, consecrated with religious ceremonies : *sacrō*, ablative of *sacrum*, religious rite (from neuter of *sacer*, sacred) + *sānctus*, past participle of *sancīre*, to consecrate.]

scapegoat (skāp′gōt′)

noun

One that is made to bear the blame of others.

verb

To make a scapegoat of.

> When things go wrong in a society, in a way and to a degree that can no longer be denied or concealed, there are various questions that one can ask. A common one, particularly in continental Europe yesterday and the Middle East today, is: "Who did this to us?" The answer to a question thus formulated is usually to place the blame on external or domestic **scapegoats** — foreigners abroad or minorities at home.
>
> — Bernard Lewis, *What Went Wrong? The Clash Between Islam and Modernity in the Middle East*, 2002

> Today, we are witnessing a replay of history. Politicians from both parties are **scapegoating** immigrants for our economic and social problems. Apparently there is a great deal of political capital in demonizing immigrants.
>
> — Raul Yzaguirre, commencement address, Mercy College, White Plains, New York, May 31, 1994

[From earlier Modern English *scape*, escape + *goat* (translation of Hebrew ʿ*ēz* ʾ*ōzēl*, goat that escapes, misreading of ʿ*ăzā'zēl*, Azazel, the evil spirit in the wilderness to whom a scapegoat was sent on the Day of Atonement according to Leviticus 16).]

꽃 *Word History:* We can lay the blame for the creation of the word *scapegoat* on an ancient misreading of the Bible. In Leviticus 16, God gives instructions for Aaron to conduct a ritual to purify the Israelites of sin on the Day of Atonement. Aaron is to take two goats, one of which he will sacrifice to God. The other is then said to be for *'ăzā'zēl.* Scholars now agree that the word *'ăzā'zēl* is the name of an evil spirit, Azazel, thought to inhabit desolate places. (The symbol ['] in *'ăzā'zēl* represents a Hebrew consonant, called *ayin,* made by constricting the throat, while the symbol ['] represents a consonant like the catch or stop in the throat in the middle of the English interjection *Uh-oh!*) Aaron is to confess the sins of the people over the second goat, and then it is to be released into the wilderness to carry these sins away to Azazel.

The Hebrew alphabet does not include a full set of symbols for writing all the vowels used in the spoken language. Instead, words are written as a series of consonants, and readers fill in the vowels mentally based on meaning and context. There is a system of marks added to the consonants to indicate all the vowels, but it was invented long after the Hebrew Scriptures were first written down. In manuscripts of the Hebrew Scriptures without vowel marks, the word for "goat," *'ēz,* is written *'z,* while *'ăzā'zēl* is written as *'z'zl.* At some point, the correct reading of *'z'zl* as *'ăzā'zēl* (the name of the demon) was forgotten, and *'z'zl* was reinterpreted as *'ēz 'ōzēl,* "goat that escapes" — a natural interpretation given the context.

This interpretation of Leviticus 16 became standard in medieval Christian tradition. In the 1530s, William Tyndale made an influential English translation of the Old Testament, and it was apparently Tyndale who created the term *scapegoat* to refer to the goat upon which Aaron put the sins of the Israelites. (*Scape* was a common variant of *escape* in Tyndale's time.) His invention caught on, and *scapegoat* eventually came to describe anyone who is made to bear the blame of others undeservedly.

spurious (spyŏŏr′ē-əs)

adjective

Lacking authenticity or validity in essence or origin; not genuine; false or fake.

> Happy is the novelist who manages to preserve an actual love letter that he received when he was young within a work of fiction, embedded in it like a clean bullet in flabby flesh and quite secure there, among **spurious** lives.
>
> — Vladimir Nabokov, *Conclusive Evidence*, 1947

[From Late Latin *spurius*, from Latin, illegitimate, probably of Etruscan origin.]

The people of my own State . . . have long since seen through the **spurious** suggestion that federal aid comes "free." They know that the money comes out of their own pockets, and that it is returned to them minus a broker's fee taken by the federal bureaucracy.

— Barry Goldwater, *The Conscience of a Conservative*, 1960

squander (skwŏn'dər)

verb

1. To spend money wastefully or extravagantly. **2.** To fail to take advantage of; lose a chance for.

> As a nation, we have been too apt to forget the benefits immigrants bring. We have also been given the opportunity to heed the lessons of our immigration history, and to this day we have **squandered** that opportunity. Instead, we have found ourselves in a desultory discourse that appeals to our worst nature as Americans, that plays to our darkest fears of "the foreigner."
>
> — Antonia Hernández, speech at Temple Isaiah, Los Angeles, CA, October 5, 1994

[Origin unknown.]

supersede (sōo′pər-sēd′)

verb

To take the place of; replace or supplant.

> From the Atlantic to the vicinity of the Rhine the Latin
> has, during many centuries, been predominant. It drove
> out the Celtic; it was not driven out by the Teutonic; and
> it is at this day the basis of the French, Spanish and Por-
> tuguese languages. In our island the Latin appears
> never to have **superseded** the old Gaelic speech, and
> could not stand its ground against the German.
>
> — Thomas B. Macaulay, *The History of England
> from the Accession of James II: Volume 1,*
> 1849–1861

> There were more gun battles, another death. Finally, a
> negotiated peace was signed. . . . The United States gov-
> ernment promised to investigate Indian affairs, and a
> presidential commission would reexamine the 1868
> treaty. The siege [of Wounded Knee, South Dakota]
> ended and 120 occupiers were arrested. The U.S. govern-
> ment then said that it had reexamined the 1868 treaty,
> found it valid, but that it was **superseded** by the U.S.
> power of "eminent domain" — the government's power to
> take land.
>
> — Howard Zinn, *A People's History of the United
> States: 1492–Present,* 1980

[From earlier Modern English *supersede*, to put a stop to (legal proceedings), annul, from Middle Scots *superceden*, to
postpone (legal proceedings), defer, from Old French *su-
perceder*, from Latin *supersedēre*, to be superior to, refrain
from : *super-*, above + *sedēre*, to sit.]

---

83 surreptitious (sûr′əp-tĭsh′əs)

adjective

Obtained or done by stealthy means; secret or clandestine.

> Sex, as an industry, is big business in this country, as it is in England. It's something everyone is deeply interested in even if only theoretically. I suppose it's always been this way, but I believe that in the old days it was discussed and practiced in a more **surreptitious** manner. However, the new school of writers have finally brought the bedroom and the lavatory out into the open for everyone to see. You can blame the whole thing on Havelock Ellis, Krafft-Ebing and Brill, Jung and Freud. (Now there's a trio for you!) Plus, of course, the late Mr. Kinsey who, not satisfied with hearsay, trundled from house to house, sticking his nose in where angels have always feared to tread.
>
> — Groucho Marx, from a letter to T. S. Eliot,
> November 1, 1963, in *The Groucho Letters:*
> *Letters from and to Groucho Marx,* 1967

[From Middle English *surrepticious*, from Latin *surreptīcius*, from *surreptus*, past participle of *surripere*, to snatch away secretly, steal : *sub-*, under, secretly + *rapere*, to seize.]

tenacity (tə-năs′ĭ-tē)

noun

1. Extreme persistence in adhering to or doing something. **2.** Unyielding existence; relentless endurance.

> Our tribe is one of the most acculturated tribes in the country, and yet there are thousands of people who still speak Cherokee. Ceremonies that we've had since the beginning of time are still going on in a tribe as acculturated as ours is. Our people are very tenacious, and it was that **tenacity** that I saw as a strength we could build on.
>
> — Wilma Mankiller, "Rebuilding the Cherokee Nation," speech at Sweet Briar College, Sweet Briar, Virginia, April 2, 1993

> It [Baltimore] is without question some of the fustiest soil in America; in the more settled classes, social styles developed in the 19th century withstand, with sporelike **tenacity**, all that the present century can throw at them. Indeed, in Baltimore all classes appear to be settled, if not cemented, in grooves of neighborhood and habit so deep as to render them impervious — as a bright child puts it in *The Accidental Tourist* — to everything except nuclear flash.
>
> — Larry McMurty, "Life Is a Foreign Country," *New York Times Book Review*, September 8, 1985

[From Latin *tenācitās*, from *tenāx, tenāc-*, holding fast, from *tenēre*, to hold.]

85 tenuous (tĕn′yoō-əs)

adjective

1. Weak or insubstantial. **2.** Having a thin consistency; dilute.

> Ironically, the Reformation would lead to greater doctrinal confusion and to the proliferation of new doctrines as the banners of the various sects which were just as rarified and **tenuous** as some of those they sought to replace.
>
> — Karen Armstrong, *A History of God: The 4000-Year Quest of Judaism, Christianity and Islam*, 1993

> The very thin and **tenuous** atmosphere of Io was found by Voyager to be composed mainly of sulfur dioxide. But this thin atmosphere can serve a useful purpose, because it may be just thick enough to protect the surface from the intense charged particles in the Jupiter radiation belt in which Io [a moon of Jupiter] is embedded.
>
> — Carl Sagan, *Cosmos*, 1980

[From Latin *tenuis*, thin, fine, slight.]

travail (trə-vāl′, trăv′āl′)

noun

1. Work, especially when arduous or involving painful effort; toil. **2.** Tribulation or agony; anguish.

> As a schoolboy ... I read that the page of history is soiled red with the blood of those who have fought for freedom. I do not know an instance in which nations have attained to their own without having to go through an incredible measure of **travail**.
>
> — Mohandas K. Gandhi, speech in England, December 1, 1931

> People with a sense of humor tend to be less egocentric and more realistic in their view of the world and more humble in moments of success and less defeated in times of **travail**.
>
> — Bob Newhart, commencement address, The Catholic University of America, Washington, DC, May 17, 1997

[From Middle English, from Old French, from *travailler*, to work hard, from Vulgar Latin **tripāliāre*, to torture with a tripalium, from Late Latin *tripālium*, a kind of instrument of torture, probably from Latin *tripālis*, having three stakes : *tri-*, three + *pālus*, stake.]

truculence (trŭk′yə-ləns)

noun

A disposition or eagerness to fight or act with bitter hostility.

> So it is proper that we assure our friends once again that, in the discharge of this responsibility, we Americans know and we observe the difference between world leadership and imperialism; between firmness and **truculence**; between a thoughtfully calculated goal and spasmodic reaction to the stimulus of emergencies.
>
> — Dwight D. Eisenhower, first inaugural address, January 20, 1953

[From Latin *truculentia,* ferocity, from *truculentus,* fierce, from *trux, truc-,* harsh, fierce.]

88 turpitude (tûr′pĭ-to͞od′)

noun

Immorality; baseness.

> We have a new television reality program about people getting into a pit with rats, which has given profound satisfaction to our public scolds. This further evidence that we are on the high road to moral rot and intellectual **turpitude** gives great satisfaction to those who are fond of denouncing Americans as a bunch of hopeless louts.
>
> — Molly Ivins, "Our Great, Weird Nation," Creators Syndicate, July 4, 2001

[From Middle English *turpytude*, from Old French, from Latin *turpitūdō*, from *turpis*, shameful.]

tyro (tī′rō)

noun

A beginner in learning something.

> A painful and frequent error among **tyros** is breaking the comic line with a too-big laugh, then a letdown; or with a laugh which is out of key or irrelevant. The masters could ornament the main line beautifully; they never addled it.
>
> — James Agee, "Comedy's Greatest Era," *Life*, September 3, 1949

[From Medieval Latin *tȳrō*, squire, variant of Latin *tīrō*, young soldier, recruit, beginner.]

unbridled (ŭn-brī′dəld)

adjective

Unrestrained; uncontrolled.

> **Unbridled** capitalism is an awesome force that creates new factories, wealth and opportunities that go first to society's risk takers and holders of capital. But unbridled capitalism is also an awesome destructive force. . . . It makes men and women obsolete as rapidly as it does the products they produce and the plants that employ them. And the people made obsolete and insecure are workers, employees, "Reagan Democrats," rooted people, conservative people who want to live their lives and raise their families in the same neighborhoods they grew up in.
>
> — Patrick J. Buchanan, "The Irreconcilable Crisis of Conservatism?" www.buchanan.org, March 23, 1998

[From Middle English *unbrydled* : *un-*, not + *bridled* (past participle of *bridelen*, to bridle, restrain, from Middle English *bridel*, bridle, from Old English *brīdel*).]

91 uncanny (ŭn-kăn′ē)

adjective

Strange or mysterious, especially in an unsettling way.

> I tried to learn from her. Not about cooking. Her Jell-O Surprise was frightening and her meatloaf worse. And it was impossible to write as she did. It was a truth universally acknowledged, as her idol Jane Austen wrote, that nobody could write with the sense and sensibility, the luminous prose and legendary reporting, of Mary McGrory.
>
> But I emulated her other talents: Her **uncanny** ability, even in remote parts of New Hampshire or Ireland, to find some sucker to carry her bags or drive her car.
>
> — Maureen Dowd, "A Star Columnist," *New York Times,* December 26, 2004

[From Scots *uncanny* : *un-*, not + *canny,* shrewd, cautious, lucky to deal with, safe (now obsolete in the last two senses), from *can,* to be able, or *can,* knowledge, skill, akin to English *can,* to be able.]

urbane (ûr-bān′)

adjective

Polite, refined, and often elegant in manner.

> As among professional politicians, so also as regards incumbents and aspirants for academic office, it is not at all unusual, nor does it cause surprise, to find such persons visibly affected with those characteristic pathological marks that come of what is conventionally called "high living" — late hours, unseasonable vigils, surfeit of victuals and drink, the fatigue of sedentary ennui. A flabby habit of body, hypertrophy of the abdomen, varicose veins, particularly of the facial tissues, a blear eye and a colouration suggestive of bile and apoplexy, — when this unwholesome bulk is duly wrapped in a conventionally decorous costume it is accepted rather as a mark of weight and responsibility, and so serves to distinguish the pillars of **urbane** society.
>
> — Thorstein Veblen, T*he Higher Learning in America,* 1918

[From Latin *urbānus*, of a city, from *urbs, urb-,* city.]

velleity (vĕ-lē′ĭ-tē)

noun

A modest wish; an inclination.

> I remember during the protest period in the 70s appearing as commencement speaker at Gettysburg College. The student leader who spoke before me used up a good part of his allotted time to distribute placards to the class betokening in single words written large, "Truth," "Love," "Peace," and other **velleities**. Mostly for my own amusement I devoted my column that evening to his performance. Four days later I got from him my column as it appeared in his local paper. He had scrawled over it in broad red ink, "Your speech wasn't all that good" which permitted me to reply that his comment was in the Gettysburg tradition of failing to notice great orations.
>
> — William F. Buckley, Jr., speech at the 50th anniversary gala of the Intercollegiate Studies Institute, October 2003

[From New Latin *velleitās*, from Latin *velle*, to want, wish.]

venial (vē′nē-əl)

adjective

Easily excused or forgiven; pardonable.

> I believe I drank too much wine last night at Hurstbourne; I know not how else to account for the shaking of my hand today. You will kindly make allowance therefore for any indistinctness of writing, by attributing it to this **venial** error.
>
> — Jane Austen, from a letter to Cassandra Austen, November 20, 1800

[From Middle English *venial*, from Old French, from Late Latin *veniālis*, from Latin *venia*, kindness, forgiveness, akin to Latin *venerārī*, to adore, venerate, and *Venus*, the goddess of love.]

verbose (vər-bōsʹ)

adjective

Using or containing a great and usually an excessive number of words; wordy.

> A democracy like ours needs a certain good humor to keep bumping along. Government as a profession tends to attract people who have a lot of time to kill and the proceedings of government tend to be long and **verbose**. And a democracy, of course, always welcomes the people's complaints, and the people who do come and complain exaggerate their complaints in hopes of getting action. So there is a lot of grimness around in a democracy. And without some good humor, government would not be able to come to work in the morning.
>
> — Garrison Keillor, speech before the National Press Club, April 7, 1994

[From Middle English *verbous* (attested only in the adverb *verbously,* loquaciously), from Latin *verbōsus,* from *verbum,* word.]

Legal language is not inherently **verbose** or compact; the incentives under which lawyers operate make all the difference. Lawyers who draft private documents, like contracts, deeds, and wills, are normally paid by the hour and may feel a need to impress their clients — or justify their fees — with the length and complexity of their prose. They are thus naturally inclined towards liberal use of redundancy and a verbose style. . . . In contrast, judges who must read aloud jury instructions, or who have to wade through a protracted "brief," have exactly the opposite incentive. Unnecessarily long documents waste their valuable time.

— Peter M. Tiersma, *Legal Language, University of Chicago Press,* 1999

96 **vexation** (věk-sā′shən)

noun

A source of irritation or annoyance.

> I miss you very much indeed; think of you at night when the world's nodding, nid, nid, nodding — think of you in the daytime when the cares of the world, and its continual **vexations** choke up the love for friends in some of our hearts; remember your warnings sometimes — try to do as you told me sometimes — and sometimes conclude it's no use to try.
>
> — Emily Dickinson, from a letter to Abiah Root, January 29, 1850

[From Old French *vexation*, from Latin *vexātiō, vexātiōn-,* from *vexāre,* to agitate.]

vista (vĭs′tə)

noun

1. A distant view or prospect, especially one seen through an opening, as between rows of buildings or trees. **2.** An awareness of a range of time, events, or subjects; a broad mental view.

> I have often reflected upon the new **vistas** that reading opened to me. I knew right there in prison that reading had changed forever the course of my life. . . . My home-made education gave me, with every additional book that I read, a little bit more sensitivity to the deafness, dumbness, and blindness that was afflicting the black race in America. Not long ago, an English writer tele-phoned me from London, asking questions. One was, "What's your alma mater?" I told him, "Books."
>
> — Malcolm X with Alex Haley, *The Autobiography of Malcolm X,* 1964

[From Italian *vista,* sight, view, from feminine past participle of *vedere,* to see, from Latin *vidēre.*]

98 **wanton** (wŏn′tən)

adjective

1. Unrestrained or excessive. **2.** Sexually promiscuous; lewd.

> A large part of the history of science, especially medical science, has been a progressive weaning away from the superficial seductiveness of individual stories that seem — but only seem — to show a pattern. The human mind is a **wanton** storyteller and, even more, a profligate seeker after pattern. We see faces in clouds and tortillas, fortunes in tea leaves and planetary movements. It is quite difficult to prove a real pattern as distinct from a superficial illusion. The human mind has to learn to mistrust its native tendency to run away with itself and see pattern where there is only randomness.
>
> — Richard Dawkins, *A Devil's Chaplain: Reflections on Hope, Lies, Science, and Love*, 2003

> The dismantling of feminism in popular culture began long ago, but on television, at least, "Real World" on MTV was a bellwether. When it began in 1992, that voyeuristic show took the music video images of **wanton** women out of the realm of MTV fantasy and into the reality genre, training cameras on the carnal pursuits of ordinary people and teaching teenagers that fame, however fleeting, trumps shame.
>
> —Alessandra Stanley, "When Creatures of 'Quality Television' Try the Opposite Approach," *New York Times*, June 3, 2004

[From Middle English *wantowen*, undisciplined : *wan-*, not, lacking (from Old English, akin to Modern English *wane*) + *towen*, past participle of *teen*, to bring up (from Old English *tēon*, to lead, draw, akin to German *ziehen*).]

wheedle (hwēd′l)

verb

1. To persuade or attempt to persuade by flattery or guile; cajole. **2.** To obtain through the use of flattery or guile.

> None of the means of information are more sacred, or have been cherished with more tenderness and care by the settlers of America, than the press. . . . Be not intimidated, therefore, by any terrors, from publishing with the utmost freedom, whatever can be warranted by the laws of your country; nor suffer yourselves to be **wheedled** out of your liberty by any pretences of politeness, delicacy, or decency.
>
> — John Adams, "A Dissertation on the Canon and Feudal Law," 1765

> The office upstairs was ceaselessly besieged by a crowd of people who were demanding rifles and being told that there were none left. The younger militia boys, who seemed to regard the whole affair as a kind of picnic, were prowling round and trying to **wheedle** or steal rifles from anyone who had them. It was not long before one of them got my rifle away from me by a clever dodge and immediately made himself scarce.
>
> — George Orwell, *Homage to Catalonia,* 1952

[Perhaps akin to Old English *wǣdlian,* to beg (from *wǣdl,* poverty) or from a source akin to German *wedeln,* to wag (the tail), fawn.]

yammer (yăm/ər)

verb

To talk continuously and often loudly.

> Sometimes the broadcast media serves the written word, as in documentaries, which are scripted so that a writer either reads what he or she has written, reports, comments about his or her own work, or is asked to comment on a topic on which, clearly, he or she has a certain specific and unique expertise. But the real glory in the industry today seems to stem from something else entirely — personality-based punditry, or the ability to **yammer** on endlessly about whatever happens to be coming down the pike.
>
> — Glenn Stout, *Best American Sports Writing 2004*

[Alteration (perhaps influenced by Middle Dutch *jammeren*, to lament, whine) of Middle English *yomeren*, to lament, wail in sorrow, groan, from Old English *geōmrian*, from *geōmr*, sorrowful, akin to German *Jammer*, lamentation, misery.]

Index of Quotations

O'Rourke, P. J.
nonchalance
Orwell, George *wheedle*
Pinker, Steven *interpolate*
Pollitt, Katha *furtive*
Post, Emily *etiquette*
Prescott, William
Hickling *consign*
Putnam, Robert D.
mawkish
Reagan, Ronald
intemperate
Rhodes, Richard *inure*
Richardson, Louise
hallmark, rankle
Roosevelt, Eleanor
imperturbable
Roosevelt, Franklin D.
bulwark, galling
Sacks, Oliver *culpable*
Sagan, Carl *tenuous*
Schama, Simon *affinity*
Schlesinger, Arthur, Jr.
juggernaut
Schwartz, Lynne Sharon
amenable
Scott, A. O.
pompous
Sen, Amartya *penury*
Simmons, Ruth *dissipate*
Smith, Adam *bauble*
Soros, George *amoral*

Stanley, Alessandra
wanton
Stiglitz, Joseph E.
nefarious
Stout, Glenn *yammer*
Sumner, Gregory D.
cosmopolitan
Tiersma, Peter M. *verbose*
Tuchman, Barbara W.
pusillanimous
Tutu, Desmond *obdurate*
Twain, Mark *depravity,*
pernicious
Veblen, Thorstein *urbane*
Vendler, Helen *patina*
Vidal, Gore *respite*
Vowell, Sarah *pompous*
Washington, George *ken*
Weber, Bruce
happenstance
Wiesel, Elie *elicit*
Wilson, Edmund
amelioration
Wilson, Edward O.
maven
Wollstonecraft, Mary
affectation, epithet
Wooden, John *gratuitous*
Woolf, Virginia *gloat*
Yergin, Daniel *propensity*
Yzaguirre, Raul *scapegoat*
Zinn, Howard *supersede*

The 100 Words

adamant
affectation
affinity
allay
amelioration
amenable
amoral
assuage
bauble
beguile
beset
bulwark
busybody
complacent
concomitant
consign
contend
cosmopolitan
culpable
depravity
derelict
dissimulate
dissipate
distill
dogmatic
elicit
epithet
espouse
expediency
forestall
furtive
galling
gloat
gratuitous

hallmark
happenstance
ignominious
imperturbable
ingratiate
innocuous
intemperate
interpolate
inure
jingoism
juggernaut
ken
latent
legacy
ludicrous
mandate
maven
mawkish
modus operandi
nefarious
nicety
nonchalance
obdurate
orthodoxy
palliate
patina
penury
pernicious
perpetuate
pittance
pompous
precipitate
prescience
profusion

propensity
pugnacity
pusillanimous
quip
rankle
reconciliation
resiliency
respite
riposte
sacrosanct
scapegoat
spurious
squander
supersede
surreptitious
tenacity
tenuous
travail
truculence
turpitude
tyro
unbridled
uncanny
urbane
velleity
venial
verbose
vexation
vista
wanton
wheedle
yammer